CRAZYSHOT!

Creative Overshot Weaving
on the Rigid Heddle Loom

Myra Wood

A Woodworks Editions book
www.myrawood.com

© 2021, Myra Wood, Woodworks Editions

First printing: July 2021
ISBN: 978-0-9800182-7-1

Editing by Sarah Peasley
Book and cover design, illustration and charts, photography: Myra Wood
e-mail: myra@woodworksart.com
www.myrawood.com

Contents

Introduction

Simple sets of repeating needlework patterns soothe my soul and keep me sane.

I love needlework that uses charts, like beading, colorwork, and lace knitting. But after one particularly grueling project with tiny knitting needles and sock-weight yarn, I realized I needed to find something equally engaging that was easier on my aching hands.

I remembered my rigid heddle loom, got it out, and immediately started to warp it. Plain weave was fine, but was too much like knitting stockinette stitch – too boring to keep my interest. I can spend hours on end on simple crafts, but what I'm really excited about are the "what-ifs?" – the experimentation – the changing patterns on the fly just to see what happens. "Just one more row" quickly becomes "just one more repeat," and before long images emerge that make me truly happy and satisfied. (Yep, I'm a cheap date.)

I looked into overshot patterns for the rigid heddle loom, and found that most involved two or more heddles, and more complicated warping than I was interested in doing at the time.

I stumbled on a traditional Russian form of weaving called Branoe in one of Kelly Casanova's wonderful videos:
  kelly-casanova-weaving-lessons.teachable. com
It had all the hallmarks I love so much about simple needlework charts, and it could be done with just one heddle and one pick-up stick.

I launched an investigation and found very little explanation other than a few basic charts on Pinterest and YouTube. I started experimenting on my own, combining the basic Branoe technique with Fair Isle knitting charts, and many of them worked! My brain was now whirling with all the different types of needlework charts I could adapt for this technique. Eventually I found myself studying more challenging charts meant for embroidery and started down a rabbit hole of modifying traditional designs.

I'm passionate about preserving traditional forms of needlework which have often been forgotten or ignored. Supplementary weft techniques are common the world over, with some references dating back to the late Roman Empire and Egypt. Latin American brocades, Branoe and branded weaving from Russia and Eastern Europe, Scandinavian Skillbragd and Krabba inlay techniques, Songket from Southeast Asia, traditional Slavic and Ukrainian weaves often used for belts, and American overshot coverlets from the 18th century all create a similar fabric structure using variations of decorative supplementary weft over a plain background. Many of these techniques even have motifs in common, despite being separated by great distance and time, most likely due to human migration.

What all of these techniques have in common is the addition of a decorative pattern using supplementary weft floats while simultaneously weaving a plain background cloth. These patterns are usually accomplished with preset warps through multiple heddles, or pick-up sticks set up in advance. The overall pattern is decided before the fabric is woven, and the initial set-up is usually very time consuming and limits the variety of patterns.

For this reason many fabrics are created with the same overall patterning.

There are techniques that use a more freeform approach, like the figurative works from Peru, Mexico, and Guatemala, as well as many from India called weft float patterns. These fabrics usually include individual figures or animals and are done with a discontinuous supplementary weft.

A distinction can be made for color changes across a row, between continuous

supplementary wefts, where the pattern weft continues from selvedge to selvedge, and discontinuous supplementary wefts, where the pattern weft only travels across a portion of the row. The method of weaving used in this book is continuous weft, most similar to Branoe weaving. A wide variety of traditional patterns have been adapted from many sources, with the addition of creative color choices.

Basic weave structure

Clearly based on the overshot weaving structure, the fabric is comprised of a plain background fabric (the "tabby") with a decorative pattern sitting on top of both sides of the fabric. Because the pattern weft appears above the background fabric via the use of floats crossing over and under the warp threads, the two sides of the fabric have opposing patterns, essentially creating a reversible fabric.

Some motifs may require longer weft floats above or below the warp threads, but this is usually kept to a minimum within the overall pattern design. Horizontally, most pattern floats cover fewer than seven warp threads. Vertically, because the alternating rows of tabby in the background fabric secure the threads with "binding points" or tie-down threads, there is no limit to the number of floats possible from row to row, but designs are typically placed along a diagonal to create a well-interwoven fabric.

Since the fabric is weft based, the overall pattern will appear to be slightly shorter when woven than it appears in the chart, but much of that has to do with the thicknesses of the yarns used and will be discussed in the section on materials.

The pattern weft yarn is typically two to three times thicker than the warp and tabby weft yarns that create the background, which helps the pattern stand out above the plain background. The background fabric is more weft-faced than a balanced weave, which also helps to distinguish the pattern from the background, giving the fabric an embossed look.

In many cases, the pattern weft covers approximately equal amounts of warp on each side. If the pattern weft includes a lot of long floats, you may prefer the look of one side over the other.

Color is an important factor to consider when planning the fabric. Branoe weaving is traditionally a red pattern on a white background.

The more contrast the pattern yarn has from the plain background (or "tabby") yarn, the better the pattern will show. Pattern colors that are close in value or hue to the tabby yarn will tend to produce a more subtle effect.

For a completely textural effect the same color can be used for all yarns.

Because fabrics made with supplementary weft techniques tend to be thicker and firmer than plain weaves, most are used for decorative home goods. These fabrics may not be suitable for clothing, where drape is a concern, but can be used as beautiful borders.

Crazyshot also works wonderfully for scarves and other accessories.

Materials

Loom

Any 20" or larger rigid heddle loom will work for all the projects included in this book. Some projects, like the mug rugs and coasters, can be done on 10" looms as indicated in the instructions. It is possible to use a frame loom, but I find a shedding mechanism helps tremendously with the tabby rows. The warp on the loom needs to be firm when weaving.

Warp yarns

After trying various combinations, I've stumbled onto my favorite yarns to use for this supplementary weft method. Any 3/2 cotton works well for the warp. 8/4 cotton will also work, but may be too thin to support some wefts. Size 3 crochet cotton is okay but is a bit too mercerized and shiny. I like Valley Yarns 3/2 mercerized cotton or Silk City 3/2 perle cotton best. You can also use rug warp, but the colors are usually limited to black and white or off-white. Fingering-weight merino wool sock yarn works, but tends to create a softer fabric, and doesn't stand up to beating as well as cotton.

Weft yarns for tabby

Tabby, or plain weave, is the simplest of weaving structures, where the weft crosses over and under alternating warp threads across a row. A gentle weft-faced weave is desirable, with very little space between rows in order to keep the pattern continuous. It doesn't need to be packed as tight as tapestry or Krokbragd, and you will see a bit of warp in the pattern areas, but the fabric shouldn't be a balanced weave.

The sweet spot for the tabby weft is a wool or wool blend sport-weight or light DK-weight yarn. My favorites are Brown Sheep Nature Spun Sport, Lambspride Superwash Sport and Knitpicks Wool of the Andes Sport. Check out yarnsub.com for substitutions. You can use the same cotton as the warp but it's not as pliable and doesn't bloom or full as much when wet-finished. Fingering or sock-weight wool yarns tend to be too thin and need to be doubled.

Weft yarns for pattern

For the pattern to show well, the pattern weft yarn needs to be at least two to three times heavier than the tabby weft yarn. Worsted-weight wool or wool blend yarns work best with a 3/2 warp and a sport-weight tabby. Acrylic yarns are an option but don't bloom and blend as well as wool does when wet finished. The pattern yarn should sit on the top of the tabby background without allowing much of the tabby to show between two adjacent pattern rows. Knit-picks Wool of the Andes comes in tons of colors and wet finishes beautifully, but there are many other yarns that work just as well: Cascade Yarns Cascade 220, Berroco Ultra Wool, Patons Classic Wool Worsted, and Brown Sheep Nature Spun Worsted, to name a few. Check out yarnsub.com for substitutions

Pick-up sticks

Make sure your stick is a bit longer than the width of your project on the loom. Because you thread the stick in and out every other row, it's helpful for it to have a smooth edge. For pick-up stitches with a ledge, I file the underside to smooth the transition and make it easier to insert without snagging on the warp.

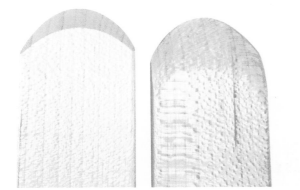

Typical pick-up with ledge on left and ledge filed down on right.

My favorite sticks are sold on Etsy by Haulin-HoofFarmStore. They have a nice pointy end and are polished smooth. They're also a bit wider than most at 1.5", which makes it much easier to throw the shuttle.

Shuttles

I prefer boat shuttles for the tabby yarn, but I prefer stick shuttles for the pattern yarn when changing colors often. I use a stick shuttle approximately the width of the project, and measure and wind on the amount of yarn needed for the rows I'll weave. If the pattern yarn is the same throughout the project, I'll use a second boat shuttle for the pattern yarn instead.

Other stuff

A good magnetic board and strip magnet are essential for following the charts. I work from the bottom up, only exposing the next row when I'm ready to weave it. That way, I always know what row I'm on. When working mirrored charts from the top down I reverse this instruction.

I use a size 14 or 16 blunt-point tapestry needle for hemstitching.

I prefer to use a fringe twister for twisted fringe, but it can also be twisted by hand.

If I want a firmer fabric or when I'm using cotton yarns, I'll often use a tapestry beater to lightly pack the weft after a few rows. The best way to decide is to try a sample at the beginning of your project before starting the actual fabric, to see what you prefer.

You can use a smaller 8"-10" loom to sample lots of options before beginning a piece on a larger loom.

I use a temple for wider fabrics. You don't need to invest in one but it makes weaving a consistent width much easier.

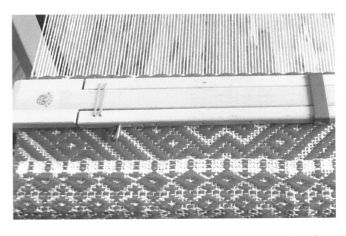

A temple is inserted from side to side to maintain the width of the weaving throughout the project.

Basic Instructions

Crazyshot is a supplementary weave, which means that a pattern is created on top of a background fabric by weaving alternating rows of two yarns; one thick, for the pattern, and one thin, for the plain background (the "tabby"). The weft for the tabby rows should match the color and weight of the warp, and can be the same thread. The weft for the pattern rows is usually at least twice as thick as the warp and tabby thread.

Charts represent the rows of pattern weft only. They are read from right to left, with each column corresponding to each warp thread, and from bottom to top, in the direction of the weaving. Tabby rows are not included in the charts and are assumed to alternate as for a normal plain weave.

Traditionally, for a set pattern of warp and weft floats done with pick-up sticks, the sticks are typically positioned and then left in place behind the heddle, requiring you to stretch your arms each time you need to manipulate them. Crazyshot is much simpler. The pick-up stick is removed after each pattern pick, and is easy to replace for each new pattern row, close to the previously woven fabric in front of the heddle. No stretching!

To start a Crazyshot pattern on a rigid heddle loom, the pick-up stick is inserted in front of the heddle while the heddle is in the neutral position. For a frame loom, the pick-up stick is inserted over or under the corresponding threads across the pattern row. For either loom, once the pick-up stick is in its proper position, it is turned on its side to create the shed, and the shuttle with the thicker pattern

yarn passes through that space.

While the heddle is in neutral position, a pick-up stick is inserted according to the chart for the pattern rows. Dark squares on the chart indicate that the pick-up stick is to go over the warp thread; for light squares the pick-up stick goes under the warp thread. After the pick is done, the stick is used to gently beat the pattern row in place, and then is removed for the next tabby pick.

Next is a tabby row. Do a tabby row after every row of pattern. When using an especially thin yarn, or a yarn that compresses a lot (like wool), you may want to do two rows of tabby between the pattern rows – this will keep the pattern more elongated vertically.

After the tabby row, use the shuttle to gently beat the tabby row into position. Some threads create more room between each pick and may need to be gently moved into place with a tapestry comb every six to eight inches. How firmly you beat the fabric is up to you, but you don't need to beat it too firmly. The pattern should be continuous vertically, without a lot of background showing between each pattern row. If you are using a frame loom, it is much easier to weave the background fabric by using a heddle bar to change the shed for the tabby rows.

This process of alternating pattern and tabby continues until the chart has been completed.

Color changes can easily be made in the pattern by adding new yarns as you weave, and wrapping the ends over the selvedge and back into the same shed over 3-4 inches of warp.

Keep an eye on the fell line and keep it as even as possible to create a consistent pattern. You can use the pick-up stick to gently beat the pattern into place, and then pack it more with the next tabby pick.

I like to use a piece of white paper under the loom while inserting the pick-up stick to make it easier to see the warp. Good lighting helps, too.

Mistakes can easily happen when trying to follow the chart and insert the pick-up stick at the same time. It's not fun to have to un-weave several rows after spotting a mistake made earlier on. Look for visual repetitions across each row so you can work intuitively, instead of reading each square on the chart as you pick up the warp threads across the row. Double-check the picked-up threads against the chart before inserting the pattern yarn. Before weaving the next tabby pick, visually compare your weaving to the chart and to the previous rows, to make sure the pattern remains correct.

You'll find, as I still do, that every once in awhile you will need to unweave a pattern pick which has been placed incorrectly. To unweave, reinsert the pick-up stick following the weave structure of the incorrect row, take out that pick, then reinsert the pick-up stick following the correct pattern.
If you've tried more than once and it still looks incorrect, look back a few rows to see if the mistake happened earlier.

Because the Crazyshot style of weaving draws the side edges in a bit more than a plain weave, it's very important to leave a slightly looser than usual edge loop on the pattern rows so that draw-in can be min-imized. A taut warp is best to achieve a smooth fabric. Tighten enough so there is no slack.

Make sure to angle the weft yarns at a 45 degree angle before beating to reduce any tightness across the fabric. Get in the habit of gently stretching the sides of the fabric outward.

Selvedges

Warp two more threads than required for the EPI (ends per inch) of the project for the selvedges; one at the beginning and one at the end. These selvedges help to anchor both sides of the patterning, since some pattern repeats may begin or end with an awkward number of weft floats across a pick. Selvedges are never included in the pattern charts.

Make sure that the pattern yarn wraps around the selvedge thread at the beginning of each row before inserting the shuttle into the shed.

Unlike most color changes in weaving, the two different yarns look best if they aren't interlocked at the edges; think of the back-ground as one fabric, with the pattern sitting on top. An easy way to make this happen is as follows: When exiting the shed and changing yarns, always place the tabby shuttle above the pattern shuttle, or the pattern shuttle below the tabby shuttle.

Charts

Charts are the backbone of the supplementary weft method of weaving.

All charted designs are worked from bottom to top initially. Some charts mirror by working from the top back down to the bottom. This will be indicated in the instructions.

Each square across a horizontal row represents one warp thread. A light square indicates that the pick-up stick goes UNDER the warp thread; a dark square indicates that the pick-up stick goes OVER the warp thread.

If you are right-handed, read each chart row and insert the pick-up stick from right to left; if you are left-handed, read each chart row and insert the pick-up stick from left to right.

In many cases, the chart will show just one pattern multiple that will be repeated across the row between the selvedge threads. If you can find a repeating over/under pattern within a row that can be easily memorized, that will help with the placement of the pickup-stick.

Your heddle is placed in the neutral position when inserting the pick-up stick. Don't worry about which side of the weaving your shuttle is on while placing the stick.

Once the pick-up stick has been inserted according to the charted pattern, the weft yarn will cross the warps correctly regardless of the side you enter from.

As you work your way through the chart, cover the upcoming chart rows with a plain

piece of paper, revealing only the row(s) that have been completed and the row that you're currently working on, so what you see on the chart matches what you see on the loom. I prefer to use a magnetic board with a magnetic strip placed above the current row. That strip doesn't move until I've finished a row and am ready to begin the next.

When your shuttle runs out of tabby weft yarn, add a new tabby yarn in the middle of a row or several warps threads in from either side edge. Lay the old tabby tail over a warp thread and through to the back, leaving a two-inch tail. Bring the new tabby thread through to the front from the back (leaving a two-inch tail) two warp threads before the old tail, and continue across the row. The tails will be trimmed after the fabric is finished. Pattern yarns can be refreshed in the same way if the incoming and outgoing colors are the same.

If there is a block of tabby between patterns and you'll see the edges of the project, cut the pattern yarn and weave in the end, then reattach it at the beginning of the next repeat even if it's the same color. If the space between repeats is narrow, you may decide to carry the pattern yarn up the side and then, and only in this case, twist the two yarns at the sides to lock the unused pattern yarn in place.

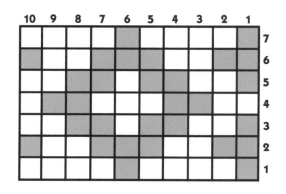

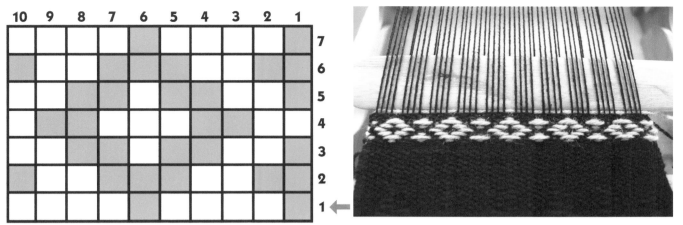

This chart shows a 10-stitch repeat. Charts do not include first and last selvedge threads.

Row 1: *1 over, 4 under, 1 over, 4 under. Repeat from * across row.

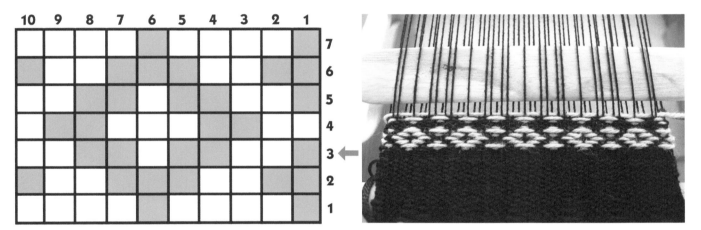

The pick-up stick is placed over the warp thread for dark squares and under the warp thread for light squares.

Row 3: *1 over, 2 under, 2 over, 1 under, 2 over, 2 under. Repeat from * across row.

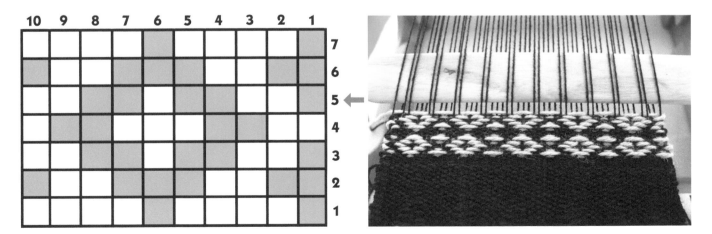

Look for obvious pattern repeats to memorize across the row. Check each row as you come to it.

Row 5: *1 over, 2 under, 2 over, 1 under, 2 over, 2 under. Repeat from * across row.

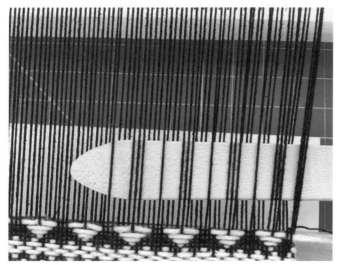

The pick-up stick is inserted in front of the heddle *in neutral position* from right to left for each row of the chart. If left-handed, reverse from left to right.

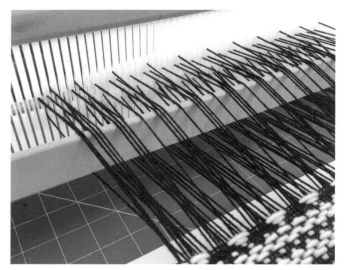

Turn the pick-up stick on its side and insert the pattern yarn at a 45 degree angle.

Make sure the pattern yarn isn't pulled too tightly.

Use the pick-up stick to gently move pattern yarn into place.

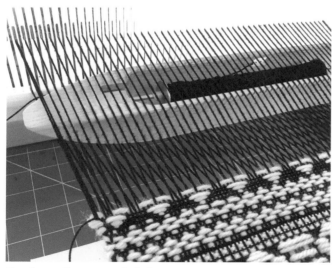

Each pattern row is followed by a tabby row.

Alternate heddle position every other tabby row.

Use your non-dominant hand to keep track as you read across the row on the chart while you insert the pick-up stick with your dominant hand.

Changing colors

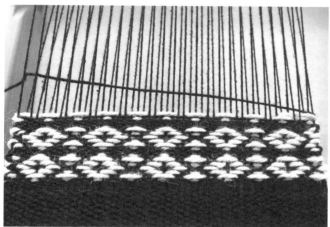

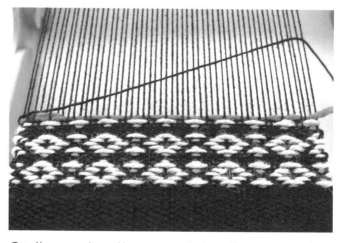

Cut the old pattern color, leaving a tail 3"-4" long. Without changing the shed, wrap the tail around the selvedge thread, back over several warp threads, and through to the back to be trimmed after wet finishing.

On the next pattern row, bring the new color through the shed from the opposite side, leaving a 3-4" tail . Without changing the shed, wrap the tail around the selvedge, back over several threads and through to the back. The doubled ends will not show in the final fabric after wet finishing.

Measure the weft yarn used across one warp width and multiply that by the number of rows for the new color, plus one extra row just to make sure there'll be enough. Wind that amount of yarn around a stick shuttle for those particular rows. I like to pre-measure and wind all the colors I'll need for a full pattern repeat.

Hemstitching

Begin or end with a tail four times the width of the fabric. For the beginning hem, first insert the needle under 2 warp threads and up 2 tabby rows and pull thread through to the front. Then insert the needle under the same 2 warp threads and out to the front along the same tabby row, through the loop of thread created between the 2 steps. Pull tightly toward the work to cinch the 2 warp threads together. For the ending hem, first insert the needle under 2 warp threads and down 2 tabby rows and pull thread through to the front, then insert the needle under the same 2 warp threads and out to the front along the same tabby row through the loop created between the 2 steps. Pull tightly toward the work to cinch the 2 warp threads together.

Fringe adds the finishing touch to your items. I like to make the fringe before wet finishing and use one of the 3 basic methods shown below.

For hemstitch alone, trim the fringe to a short, even length with a rotary cutter on a mat with a ruler.

For knotted fringe, group bundles of 4 warp threads and tie an overhand knot, sliding the knot up to the hem. Trim evenly.

Twisted fringe can be done by hand or with the aid of a nifty fringe twister. Two groups of 2 warp threads are each twisted to the right until they start twisting back on themselves, then the 2 groups are twisted together to the left to ply and hold them together. A single overhand knot at the end secures the twist at the desired length. Trim all ends evenly.

Hemstitch alone, fringe trimmed evenly.

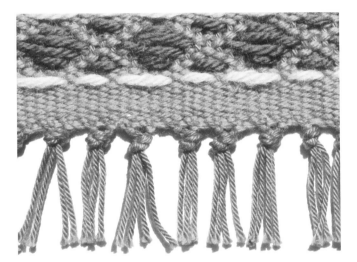

Hemstitch with knotted fringe

Wet Finishing

The fabric isn't finished until it's been wet finished. After the desired fringe is done, fill a bucket or sink with lukewarm water and a little wool wash like Soak or Eucalan. Let the fabric soak thoroughly a few minutes while gently agitating. This will help the pattern yarn blend with the tabby background. Squeeze out as much water as possible and lay flat on a towel to dry, squaring up the edges.

Hemstitch with twisted fringe

Projects

Each project begins and ends with plain sections woven with tabby yarn. Within the initial and ending plain tabby sections:

- At the beginning, leave a tabby yarn tail 4 times the width of the warp.
- Within these sections, beat tabby yarn firmly for a weft-faced weave with no warp showing.
- After initial plain tabby section has been woven, use the tabby yarn tail to hemstitch the bottom edge across 2 warp threads and up 2 weft rows.
- After the final plain tabby section has been woven, cut a tabby yarn tail 4 times the width of the warp, and use it to hemstitch the top edge across 2 warp threads and down 2 weft rows.

Each project includes one or more charts woven with the pattern yarn(s). Within these sections:

- Begin each chart at bottom right corner, reading each row from right to left, from the bottom up.
- First and last warp threads (selvedges) are not included in the charts.
- At pattern yarn color changes, wrap beginning and ending pattern yarn tails around selvedge warp threads, then weave back into the same shed.
- Color changes for some patterns are indicated in the charts, but feel free to change and rearrange the colors any way you'd like.
- Alternate the shed for each row (pattern or tabby), making sure the pattern or tabby yarn wraps around the selvedge threads.

- Follow each pattern row of the chart with a plain row of tabby yarn.
- Beat each chart row just enough to close the gap between yarns – not too hard.
- For each plain (no pattern yarn) chart row, weave 2 rows of tabby yarn.
- Within plain tabby sections between charts, beat tabby yarn firmly for a weft-faced weave with no warp showing.
- If the space between patterns is narrow, you may decide to carry the pattern yarn up the side edge. In this case, and ONLY in this case, twist the pattern and tabby yarns together at the selvedge to lock the unused pattern yarn in place.

When weaving more than one item on the same warp:

- Cut a piece of light cardboard wider than the width of the warp on the loom and slightly taller than twice the length of the fringe. Cut that piece into thirds.
- After completing one item, change the shed, place one piece of cardboard within the shed, change the shed again and place another cardboard, change the shed again and insert the last piece. Change the shed one more time, and then you are ready to proceed with the next item.

Unless otherwise specified, finish all items as follows:

- Remove fabric from loom.
- Using a rotary cutter, trim fringe to specified length.
- Hand wash and lay flat to dry.

Equipment
10" rigid heddle loom or larger with a 7.5 or 8 dent heddle, 2 or 3 shuttles, pick-up stick, tapestry needle

Yarn
Warp:
3/2 or 8/4 cotton, 60 yds (Valley Yarns Valley Cotton 3/2, Black)
Weft (tabby): Sport-weight wool or wool blend, 75 yds (Valley Yarns Valley Cotton 3/2, Black)
Weft (pattern yarn): Worsted-weight cotton, 60 yds of 1 color, or 30 yds each of 2 colors (Knitpicks Dishie, Azure and Clementine)

Sett
Warp: 7.5 epi

7.5 epi x 25 ppi = 1" tabby woven on loom

Total warp ends: 42 (40 + 2 for selvedges)

Dimensions
Width on the loom: 5"

Warp length for 4 coasters: 51" (5" + 2" for fringe per coaster, and 20" waste) (allow 3" between coasters when weaving, for fringe)

Finished size: 4.5" x 5" each, without fringe

shown in 1 and 2 color options

Weaving Instructions

Warp 42 ends.

Coaster Instructions:

With tabby yarn, weave 8 rows.
Hemstitch bottom edge.

Work chart from beginning to end, as follows:

For 1 color, cut and weave in the pattern yarn tail after the last row of the chart.

For 2 colors, change color as indicated, cutting and weaving in the pattern yarn tails when they are no longer needed.

With tabby yarn, weave 38 rows.

Work chart from beginning to end once more.

With tabby yarn, weave 8 rows.
Hemstitch top edge.

For each additional coaster, insert 3" of cardboard and repeat Coaster Instructions.

Finish, trimming fringe on each coaster to 1".

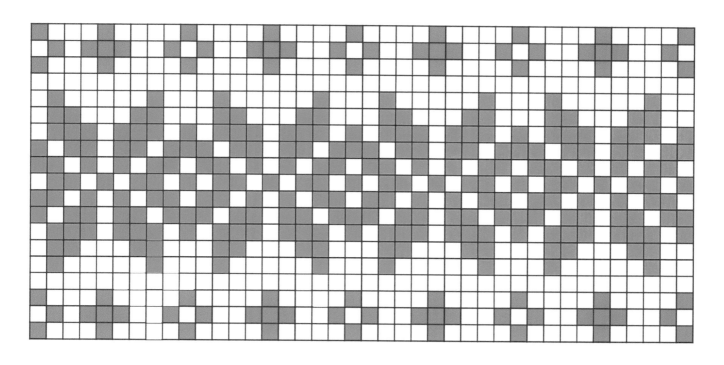

Crimson and Clover Coasters

Weaving Instructions

Warp 41 ends.

Coaster Instructions:

With tabby yarn, weave 8 rows.
Hemstitch bottom edge.

Work chart from beginning to end, cutting
and weaving in the pattern yarn tail after
the last row of the chart.

With tabby yarn, weave 8 rows.
Hemstitch top edge.

For each additional coaster, insert 3" of
cardboard and repeat Coaster Instructions.

Finish, trimming fringe on each coaster to 1".

Equipment

10" rigid heddle loom or larger with a 7.5 or 8 dent heddle, 2 shuttles, pick-up stick, tapestry needle

Yarn

Warp: 3/2 or 8/4 cotton or cotton blend, 60 yds (Valley Yarns Valley Cotton 3/2, Porcelain Blue)

Weft (tabby): Sport-weight wool or wool blend, 75 yds (Cascade Yarns Cascade 220 Sport, 9672 Ultramarine Green)

Weft (pattern yarn): Worsted-weight wool yarn, 60 yds (Knitpicks Wool of the Andes Worsted, Dragonfruit)

Sett

Warp: 7.5 epi

7.5 epi x 25 ppi = 1" tabby woven on loom

Total warp ends: 41
(39 + 2 for selvedges)

Dimensions

Width on loom: 5"

Warp length for 4 coasters: 51" (5" + 2" for fringe per coaster, and 20" waste) (allow 3" between coasters when weaving, for fringe)

Finished size: 4.5" x 5" each, without fringe

Warping an odd number of ends

To keep this pattern centered and symmetrical, an odd number of ends needs to be warped. In order to do this with direct warping, bring loops through the slots to the warping peg as usual. On the last loop, cut the warp thread at the warping peg rather than bringing back to the apron rod to tie off. The last slot will only have 1 thread instead of 2.

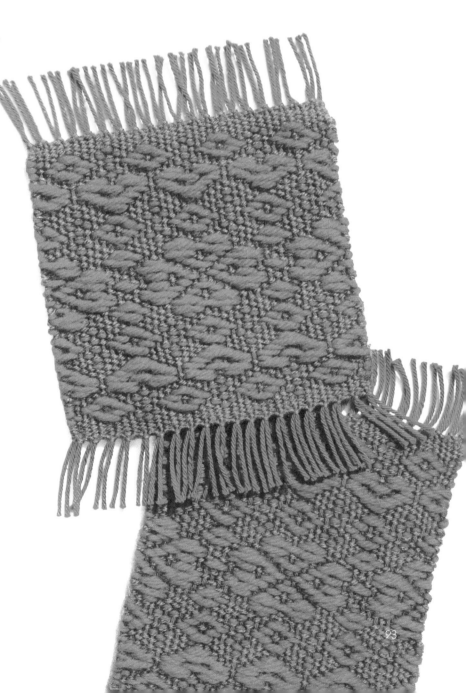

Equipment
10" rigid heddle loom or larger with a 7.5 or 8 dent heddle, 2 shuttles, pick-up stick, tapestry needle

Yarn
Warp: 3/2 or 8/4 cotton or cotton blend, 60 yds (Valley Yarns Valley Cotton 3/2, Admiral Blue)

Weft (tabby): Sport-weight wool or wool blend, 75 yds (Valley Yarns Valley Superwash Sport, Classic Navy)

Weft (pattern yarn): Worsted-weight wool yarn, 60 yds (Knitpicks Wool of the Andes Worsted, Mink Heather)

Sett
Warp: 7.5 epi

7.5 epi x 25 ppi = 1" tabby woven on loom

Total warp ends: 41 (39 + 2 for selvedges)

Dimensions
Width on the loom: 5"

Warp length for 4 coasters: 51" (5" + 2" for fringe per coaster, and 20" waste) (allow 3" between coasters when weaving, for fringe)

Finished size: 4.5" x 5" each, without fringe

Weaving Instructions

Warp 41 ends.

Coaster Instructions:

First half:

With tabby yarn, weave 10 rows. Hemstitch bottom edge.

Work chart from beginning to end, cutting and weaving in the pattern yarn tail after the last row of the chart.

Second half:

With tabby yarn, weave 1 row.

Beginning with the second row from top, work chart in reverse.

With tabby yarn, weave 10 rows. Hemstitch top edge.

For each additional coaster, insert 3" of cardboard and repeat Coaster Instructions.

Finish, trimming fringe on each coaster to 1".

opposite page: After hemstitching between each coaster, place three 1" pieces of cardboard cut 2" wider than the warp between the sheds, changing position of the heddle for each piece. This will provide plenty of room for fringe.

Follow the Band Mug Rug

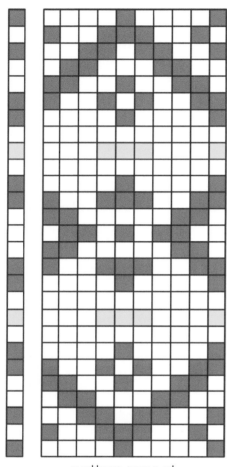

pattern repeat

Weaving Instructions

Warp 63 ends.

With tabby yarn, weave 16 rows.
Hemstitch bottom edge.

Work chart from beginning to end changing color as indicated, and cutting and weaving in the pattern yarn tails when they are no longer needed.

With tabby yarn, weave 20 rows.

Work chart from beginning to end two more times, changing colors as desired, and weaving 20 rows of tabby between charts as established.

With tabby yarn, weave 16 rows. Hemstitch top edge.

Finish, twisting fringe in 4-warp bundles, knotting ends evenly and trimming to 2".

Each line of the pattern is repeated across the row six times. The last warp, shown as the separate box to the left of the pattern repeat, is worked one time at the end of the row to mirror the opposite edge.

Mug rugs are the perfect size for a cup of tea and a couple cookies.

Equipment

10" rigid heddle loom or larger with a 7.5 or 8 dent heddle, 4 shuttles, pick-up stick, tapestry needle

Yarn

Warp: 3/2 or 8/4 cotton or cotton blend, size 3 cotton yarn, 60 yds (Valley Yarns Valley Cotton 3/2, Admiral Blue)

Weft (tabby): Sport-weight wool or wool blend, 50 yds (Cascade Yarns Cascade 220 Sport, 8393 Navy)

Weft (pattern yarn): Worsted-weight wool or wool blend, 15 yds each of 2 colors and 2 yards of accent color (Knitpicks Wool of the Andes Worsted, Red, Brass Heather, and Cloud [accent])

Sett

Warp: 7.5 epi

7.5 epi x 25 ppi = 1" tabby woven on loom

Total warp ends: 63
(61 + 2 for selvedges)

Dimensions

Width on the loom: 7"

Warp length for one mug rug: 34" (10" + 4" for fringe, and 20" for loom waste)
Add 14" to warp for each additional rug

Finished size: 6.5" x 9", without fringe

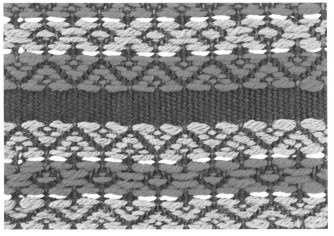

detail of reverse side

Equipment
10" rigid heddle loom or larger with a 7.5 or 8 dent heddle, 2 shuttles, pick-up stick, tapestry needle

Yarn
Warp:
3/2 or 8/4 cotton or cotton blend, size 3 cotton yarn, 60 yds (Valley Yarns Valley Cotton 3/2, Admiral Blue)
Weft (tabby):
Sport-weight wool or wool blend, 50 yds (Cascade Yarns Cascade 220 Sport, 9673 Mulberry Purple)
Weft (pattern yarn):
Worsted-weight wool or wool blend, 40 yds (Knitpicks Wool of the Andes Worsted, Magic)

Sett
Warp: 7.5 epi

7.5 epi x 25 ppi = 1" tabby woven on loom

Total warp ends: 63
(61 + 2 for selvedges)

Dimensions
Width on loom: 7"

Warp length for one mug rug:
34" (10" + 4" for fringe, and 20" for loom waste)
Add 14" to warp for each additional rug

Finished size: 6.5" x 8", without fringe

Weaving Instructions

Warp 63 ends.

With tabby yarn, weave 8 rows.
Hemstitch bottom edge.

Work chart from beginning to end once, cutting and weaving in the pattern yarn tail after the last row of the chart.

With tabby yarn, weave 8 rows.
Hemstitch top edge.

Finish, twisting fringe in 4-warp bundles, knotting ends evenly and trimming to 2".

Walk This Way Mug Rug

Weaving Instructions

Warp 63 ends.

With tabby yarn, weave 16 rows. Hemstitch bottom edge.

Work chart from beginning to end, changing color as indicated, cutting and weaving in the pattern yarn tails when they are no longer needed.

With tabby yarn, weave 16 rows. Hemstitch top edge.

Finish, knotting fringe in 4-warp bundles and trimming to 2".

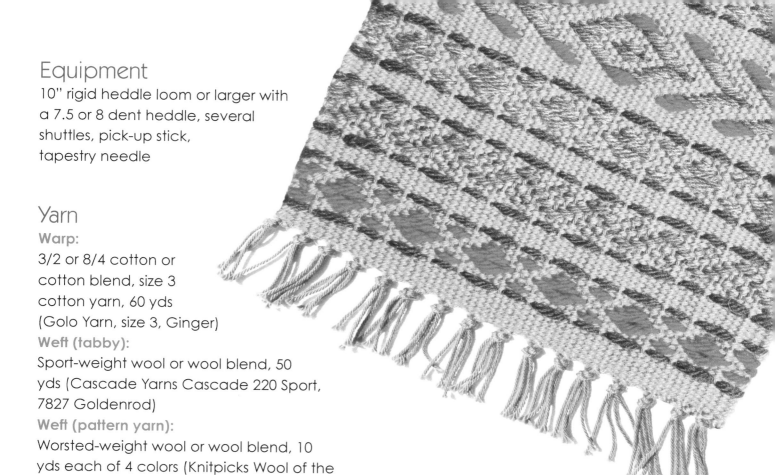

Equipment

10" rigid heddle loom or larger with a 7.5 or 8 dent heddle, several shuttles, pick-up stick, tapestry needle

Yarn

Warp:
3/2 or 8/4 cotton or cotton blend, size 3 cotton yarn, 60 yds (Golo Yarn, size 3, Ginger)
Weft (tabby):
Sport-weight wool or wool blend, 50 yds (Cascade Yarns Cascade 220 Sport, 7827 Goldenrod)
Weft (pattern yarn):
Worsted-weight wool or wool blend, 10 yds each of 4 colors (Knitpicks Wool of the Andes Worsted, Red, Whirlpool, Amethyst Heather, Thyme)

Sett

Warp: 7.5 epi

7.5 epi x 25 ppi = 1" tabby woven on loom

Total warp ends: 63
(61 + 2 for selvedges)

Dimensions

Width on the loom: 7"
Warp length for one mug rug:
34" (10" + 4" for fringe, and 20" for loom waste)
Add 14" to warp for each additional rug

Finished size: 6.5" x 9", without fringe

Weaving Instructions

Warp 115 ends.

First half:

With tabby yarn, weave 12 rows. Hemstitch bottom edge.

Carrying pattern yarn up the side edge throughout, work as follows:

Work Chart **A** from beginning to end.
With tabby yarn, weave 4 rows.
Work Chart **B** from beginning to end.
With tabby yarn, weave 4 rows.
Work Chart **C** from beginning to end.
With tabby yarn, weave 4 rows.
Work Chart **D** from beginning to end.
With tabby yarn, weave 4 rows.
Work Chart **E** from beginning to end.

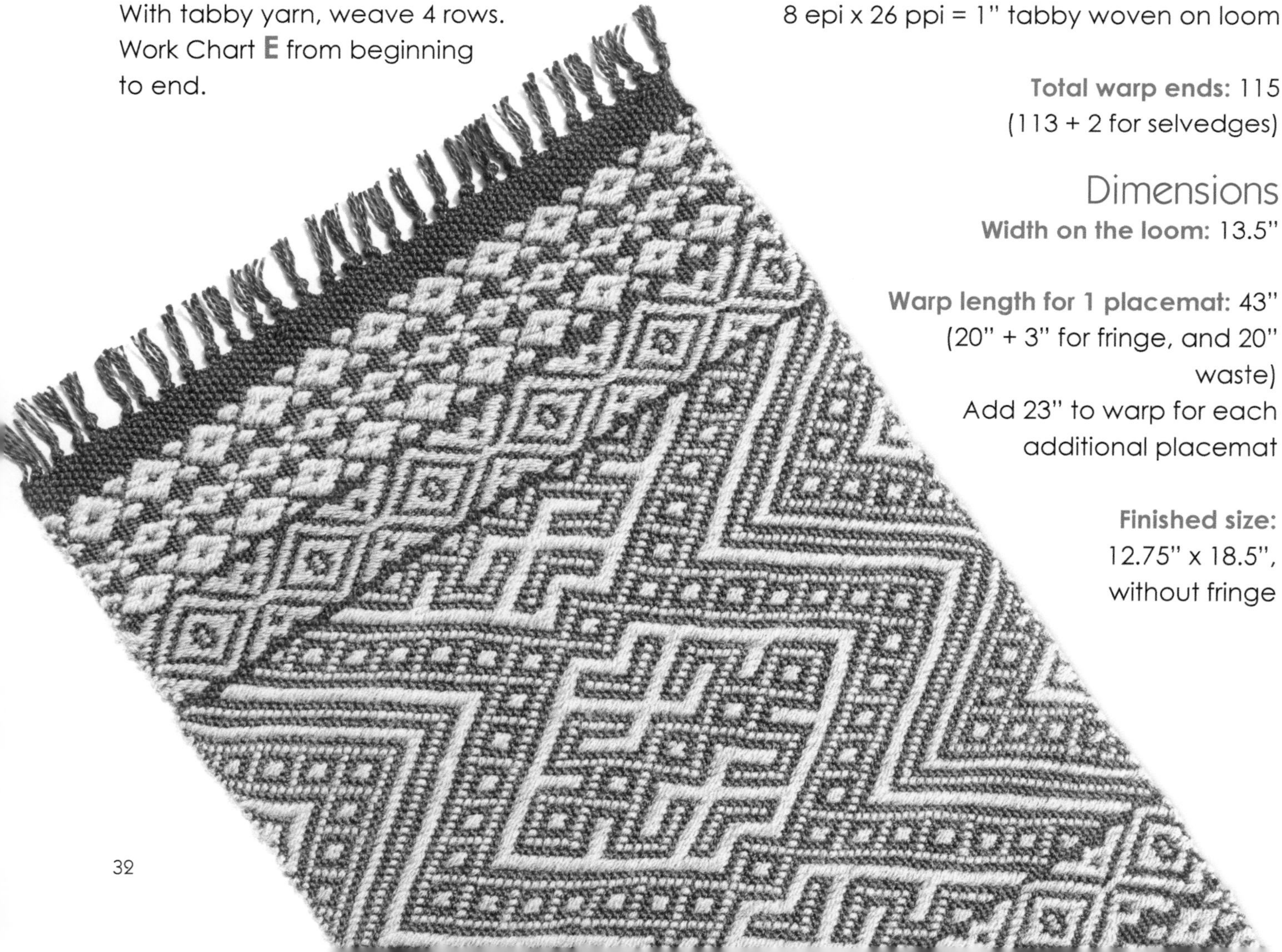

Equipment

16" rigid heddle loom or larger with a 7.5 or 8 dent heddle, 2 shuttles, pick-up stick, tapestry needle

Yarn

Warp: 3/2 or 8/4 cotton or cotton blend, 100 yds (Valley Yarns Valley Cotton 3/2, Black Forest)
Weft (tabby): Sport-weight wool or wool blend, 140 yds (Brown Sheep Nature Spun Sport, Mallard)
Weft (pattern yarn): Worsted-weight wool or wool blend, 100 yds (KnitPicks Wool of the Andes Worsted, Bamboo Heather)

Sett

Warp: 8 epi

8 epi x 26 ppi = 1" tabby woven on loom

Total warp ends: 115 (113 + 2 for selvedges)

Dimensions

Width on the loom: 13.5"

Warp length for 1 placemat: 43" (20" + 3" for fringe, and 20" waste)
Add 23" to warp for each additional placemat

Finished size: 12.75" x 18.5", without fringe

Every Which Way Placemat

Second half:

Beginning with the second row from the top, work Chart **E** in reverse (from top to bottom). With tabby yarn, weave 4 rows.
Work Chart **D** in reverse (from top to bottom). With tabby yarn, weave 4 rows.
Work Chart **C** in reverse (from top to bottom). With tabby yarn, weave 4 rows.

Work Chart **B** in reverse (from top to bottom). With tabby yarn, weave 4 rows.
Work Chart **A** in reverse (from top to bottom).

With tabby yarn, weave 12 rows. Hemstitch top edge.

Finish, knotting fringe in 4-warp bundles and trimming to 1.5".

E

D

C

B

A

Equipment
16" rigid heddle loom or larger with a 7.5 or 8 dent hedle, 2 shuttles, pick-up stick, tapestry needle

Yarn
Warp: 3/2 or 8/4 cotton or cotton blend, 125 yds (Valley Yarns Valley Cotton 3/2, Black)
Weft (tabby): Sport-weight wool or wool blend, 140 yds (Cascade Yarns Cascade 220 Sport, 9616 Fudge Brownie)
Weft (pattern yarn): Worsted-weight wool or wool blend, 100 yds (KnitPicks Wool of the Andes Worsted, Persimmon Heather)

Sett
Warp: 8 epi

8 epi x 26 ppi = 1" tabby woven on loom

Total warp ends: 122 (120 + 2 for selvedges)

Dimensions
Width on the loom: 14"

Warp length for 1 placemat: 43" (19" + 4" for fringe, and 20" waste)
Add 23" to warp for each additional placemat

Finished size:
12.75" x 17.5", without fringe

Weaving Instructions

Warp 122 ends.

With tabby yarn, weave 12 rows.
Hemstitch bottom edge.

Working each chart row six times across the warp, work Chart **A** from beginning to end once, work Chart **B** from beginning to end 4 times, then work Chart **A** from beginning to end once more.

With tabby yarn, weave 12 rows.
Hemstitch top edge.

Finish, knotting fringe in 4-warp bundles and trimming to 2".

Each pattern repeat of Chart **B** measures 3" tall. If you'd prefer a table runner, add as many sections of Chart **B** as desired and adjust the length of the warp accordingly.

Opposite side

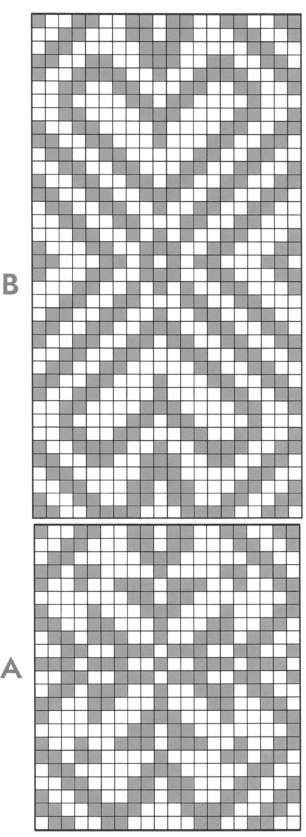

B

A

Fair Game Pillow

When changing colors:

- Weave in tails over 3 to 4 warp threads.

- No need to trim tails; they will remain on the inside of the pillow after finishing.

- If a color is to be used again within 3 to 4 pattern rows, carry it up along the side edge, catching it in the selvedge.

Equipment
20" rigid heddle loom or larger with a 7.5 or 8 dent heddle, several stick shuttles, pick-up stick, tapestry needle, 16" pillow form

Yarn
Warp: 3/2 or 8/4 cotton or cotton blend, 240 yds (Valley Yarns Valley Cotton 3/2, Black Forest)
Weft (tabby): Sport-weight wool or wool blend, 450 yds (Valley Yarns Charlemont, Black)
Weft (pattern yarn): Worsted-weight wool or wool blend, 20 yds each of 7 colors (KnitPicks Wool of the Andes Worsted, Bamboo Heather, Amethyst Heather, Ciel, Lake Ice Heather, Roobios Heather, Poet, Haze Heather)
Weft (back of pillow): Worsted-weight wool or wool blend, 175 yds (KnitPicks Wool of the Andes Worsted, Coal)

Sett
Warp: 8 epi

8 epi x 26 ppi = 1" tabby woven on loom

Total warp ends: 142 (140 + 2 for selvedge)

Dimensions
Width on the loom: 16.5"

Warp length: 55" (35" and 20" for loom waste)

Finished size: 16" x 35" (folded in half lengthwise)

Weaving Instructions

Warp 142 ends.

With tabby yarn, weave 24 rows. Hemstitch bottom edge.

Working each chart row seven times across the warp, work Chart **A** from beginning to end once, then work Chart **B** from beginning to end once.

With tabby yarn, weave 8 rows. Cut tabby yarn and weave in the tail.

Join worsted-weight yarn for back on opposite edge and plain weave 17" for back of pillow.

Hemstitch top edge.
Finish fabric.

Assembly

Where yarn changes to sport weight, fold fabric in half with right sides together.

Leaving a ¼" seam allowance, machine stitch along each side edge or whipstitch by hand. Turn pillow cover right-side out; insert pillow form.

Fold top edges including fringe to inside.

Use mattress stitch to sew folded edges together evenly.

A

B

Equipment

20" rigid heddle loom or larger with a 7.5 or 8 dent heddle, several stick shuttles, pick-up stick, tapestry needle, 16" pillow form.

Yarn

Warp: 3/2 or 8/4 cotton or cotton blend, 240 yds (Valley Yarns Valley Cotton 3/2, Black)

Weft (tabby): Sport-weight wool or wool blend, 450 yds (Valley Yarns Charlemont, Black)

Weft (pattern yarn): Worsted-weight wool or wool blend, 150 yds total of various colors (10 yds each of assorted scraps)

Weft (back of pillow): Worsted-weight wool or wool blend, 175 yds (KnitPicks Wool of the Andes Worsted, Coal)

Sett

Warp: 8 epi

8 epi x 26 ppi = 1" tabby woven on loom

Total warp ends: 142 (140 + 2 for selvedge)

Dimensions

Width on the loom: 16.5"

Warp length: 55" (35" and 20" for loom waste)

Finished size: 16" x 35" (folded in half lengthwise)

Weaving Instructions

Warp 142 ends.

With tabby yarn, weave 24 rows. Hemstitch bottom edge.

Working each chart row seven times across the warp, work Chart **A** from beginning to end once, then work Chart **B** from beginning to end once.

With tabby yarn, weave 8 rows. Cut tabby yarn and weave in the tail.

Join worsted-weight yarn for back on opposite edge and plain weave 17" for back of pillow. Hemstitch top edge. Finish fabric.

Assembly

Where yarn changes to sport weight, fold fabric in half with right sides together.

Leaving a ¼" seam allowance, machine stitch along each side edge, or whipstitch by hand. Turn pillow cover right-side out; insert pillow form.

Fold top edges including fringe to inside.

Use mattress stitch to sew folded edges together evenly.

A   **B**

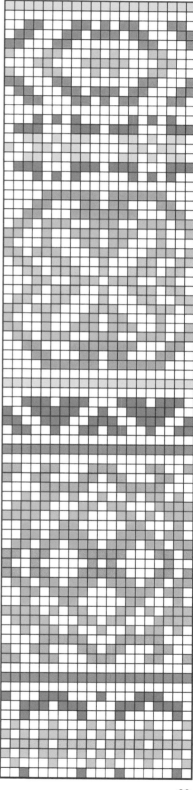

Equipment

20" rigid heddle loom or larger with a 7.5 or 8 dent heddle, several stick shuttles, pick-up stick, tapestry needle, 16" pillow form

Yarn

Warp: 3/2 or 8/4 cotton or cotton blend, 240 yds (Valley Yarns Valley Cotton 3/2, Black Forest)

Weft (tabby): Sport-weight wool or wool blend, 450 yds (Valley Yarns Charlemont, Black)

Weft (pattern yarn): Worsted-weight wool or wool blend, 20 yds each of 8 colors (Stunning String Studio, Mini-skein kit, Beachcomber)

Weft (back of pillow): Worsted-weight wool or wool blend, 175 yds (KnitPicks Wool of the Andes Worsted, Coal)

Sett

Warp: 8 epi

8 epi x 26 ppi = 1" tabby woven on loom

Total warp ends: 142 (140 + 2 for selvedge)

Dimensions

Width on the loom: 16.5"

Warp length: 55" (35" and 20" for loom waste)

Finished size: 16" x 35" (folded in half lengthwise)

She's a Rainbow Pillow

Weaving Instructions

Warp 142 ends.

With tabby yarn, weave 24 rows. Hemstitch bottom edge.

Working each chart row 14 times across the warp, work Chart **A** from beginning to end once, work Chart **B** from beginning to end once, work Chart **C** from beginning to end once, then work the first 27 rows of Chart **A** once more with purple yarn.

With tabby yarn, weave 8 rows. Cut tabby yarn and weave in the tail.

Join worsted-weight yarn for back on opposite edge and plain weave 17" for back of pillow.

Hemstitch top edge.
Finish fabric.

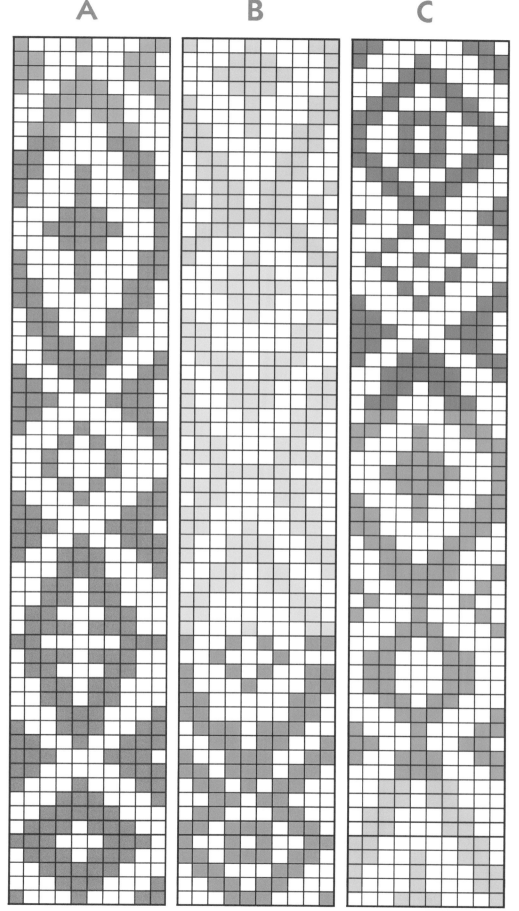

A B C

Assembly

Where yarn changes to sport weight, fold fabric in half with right sides together.

Leaving a ¼" seam allowance, machine stitch along each side edge or whipstitch by hand.

urn pillow cover right-side out; insert pillow form.

Turn top edges including fringe to inside.

Use mattress stitch to sew folded edges together evenly.

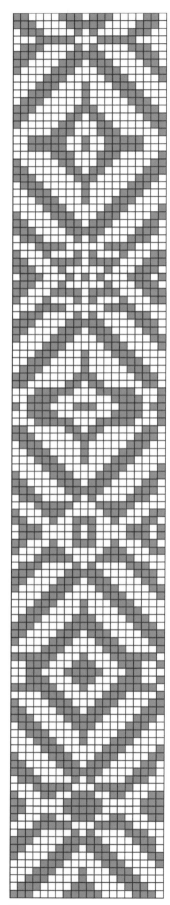

Weaving Instructions

Warp 122 ends.

With tabby yarn, weave 16 rows.
Hemstitch bottom edge.

*Working each chart row six times across the warp, work chart from beginning to end once, then work chart again in reverse (from top to bottom).

Repeat from * until weaving measures approximately 41" from hemstitch.

Cut and weave in the pattern yarn tail after the last row.

With tabby yarn, weave 16 more rows.
Hemstitch top edge.

Finish, twisting fringe in 4-warp bundles, knotting ends evenly and trimming to 4".

To keep track of the length of my weaving, I pin a tape measure just below the fell line and move it up as I weave.

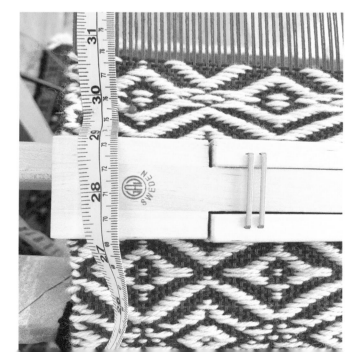

Equipment
20" rigid heddle loom or larger with a 7.5 or 8 dent heddle, 2 shuttles, pick-up stick, tapestry needle

Yarn
Warp: 3/2 or 8/4 cotton or cotton blend, 275 yds (Supreme/UKI 3/2 Pearl Cotton, 1210 Wine)

Weft (tabby): Sport-weight wool or wool blend, 250 yds (Brown Sheep Nature Spun Sport, Scarlet)

Weft (pattern yarn): Worsted-weight wool or wool blend, 250 yds (KnitPicks Wool of the Andes Worsted, Cloud)

Sett
Warp: 8 epi

8 epi x 26 ppi = 1" tabby woven on loom

Total warp ends: 122
(120 + 2 for selvedge)

Dimensions
Width on the loom: 13.75"

Warp length: 78"
(40" + 18" for fringe, and 20" waste)

Finished size:
12.5" x 40",
without fringe

Equipment
20" rigid heddle loom or larger with a 7.5 or 8 dent heddle, several stick shuttles, pick-up stick, tapestry needle

Yarn
Warp: 3/2 or 8/4 cotton or cotton blend, 230 yds (Valley Yarns Valley Cotton 3/2, Black)
Weft (tabby): Sport-weight wool or wool blend, 300 yds (Valley Yarns Charlemont, Black)
Weft (pattern yarn): Worsted-weight wool or wool blend, 43 yds each of 7 colors (KnitPicks Wool of the Andes Worsted, Magic, Roobios Heather, Pumpkin, Green Tea Heather, Lake Ice Heather, Ciel, Poet)

Sett
Warp: 8 epi

8 epi x 26 ppi = 1" tabby woven on loom

Total warp ends: 122 (120 + 2 for selvedges)

Dimensions
Width on the loom: 14"

Warp length: 66" (40" + 6" for fringe, and 20" waste)

Finished size: 12.75" x 38.5", without fringe

Marakesh Express Table Runner

Weaving Instructions

Warp 122 ends.

With tabby yarn, weave 14 rows.
Hemstitch bottom edge.

First half:

Chart **1**, (3)twt, (4)twp, (3)twt, Chart **2**, (3)twt, (2)twp, (3)twt, Chart **3**, (3)twt, Chart **4**, (14) twt, Chart **5**, (14)twt, Chart **6**, (14)twt, Chart **7**, (3)twt, (4)twp, (3)twt, Chart **8**, (3)twt, Chart **9**, (3)twt, Chart **10**, (6)twt, (2)twp, (6)twt, Chart **11**, (3)twt, Chart **12**, (3)twt, (2)twp, (3)twt, Chart **13**, (3)twt, Chart **14**, (14)twt, Chart **15**, (14)twt.

Second half:

Repeat instructions for first half.

Hemstitch top edge.
Finish fabric.

Abbreviations:

(number of rows to weave**)twt** - plain weave with tabby yarn only.

(number of rows to weave**)twp** - plain weave with pattern yarn only.

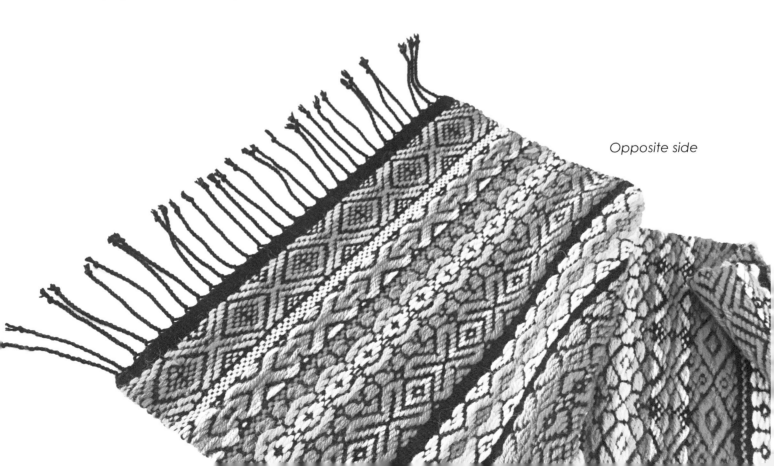

Opposite side

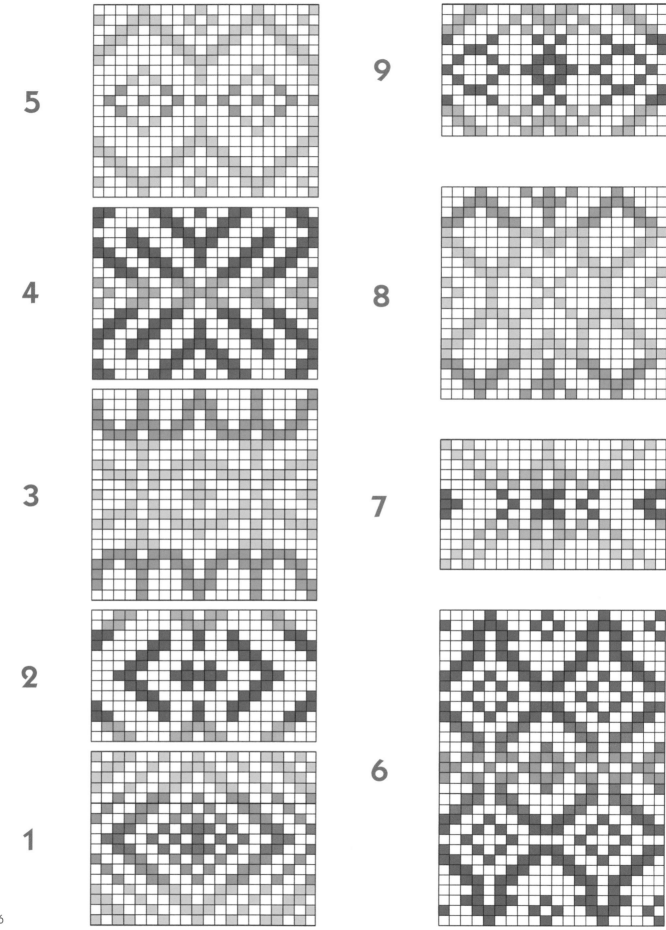

14

13

12

11

10

15

Checked Out Table Topper

Equipment

16" rigid heddle loom or larger with a 7.5 or 8 dent heddle, 2 shuttles, pick-up stick, tapestry needle

Yarn

Warp: 3/2 or 8/4 cotton or cotton blend, 160 yds (Valley Yarns Valley Cotton 3/2, Natural)

Weft (tabby): Sport-weight wool or wool blend, 120 yds (Cascade Yarns Cascade 220 Sport, 8010 Natural)

Weft (pattern yarn): Worsted-weight wool or wool blend, 120 yds (KnitPicks Wool of the Andes Worsted, Hollyberry)

Sett

Warp: 8 epi

8 epi x 26 ppi = 1" tabby woven on loom

Total warp ends: 143 (141 + 2 for selvedges)

Dimensions

Width on the loom: 16"

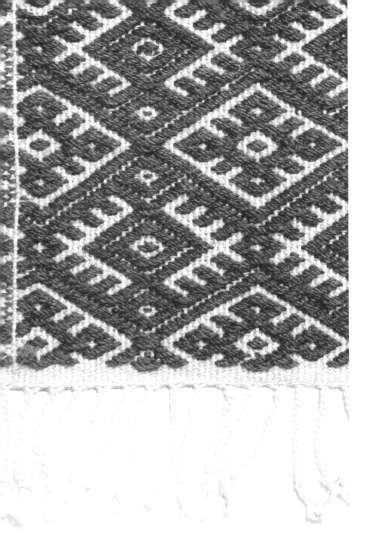

Warp length: 42" (16" + 6" for fringe, and 20" waste)

Finished size:
15.75" x 15.75",
without fringe

Weaving Instructions

Warp 143 ends.

First half:
With tabby yarn, weave 12 rows.
Hemstitch bottom edge.

Work chart from beginning to end.

Second half:
Beginning with the second row from the top, work chart in reverse (from top to bottom).

With tabby yarn, weave 12 rows. Hemstitch top edge.

Finish, twisting fringe in 4-warp bundles, knotting ends evenly and trimming to 2.5".

Enjoy your Crazyshot Adventures!